Special Thank You to my fri
parents, Mark, my 5 childrer
Yorkie friends, all of you who give your time and love to help out
in my Yorkie groups to keep them as successful as they are, and
most importantly - my babies (human and Yorkies) :)

May you all know how special you are to me.

"Everyone we meet along the way plays a part in shaping who we
become through lessons learned, memories cherished, and the
day to day joy we are blessed to experience every day" - me

Thank you to each and every one of you for all you do, and for
simply being a part of my life. Every one of you has played a
part in making this book happen in one way or another.

To Aiden, Owen, Delanie, Bella, and Cienna.......
You are the "Joy of my Life," and you each play such a
special part in what makes us the program we are
today through love, laughter, success, continual
improvement, and most importantly the blessing it is
to be your mom. You are what pushes me every day to
do better and better to give you the best life I possibly
can, even when it means the dogs get to come with us
on Vacations :). May you all use your true potential,
passion, love, and desire to achieve everything you
ever want in life, times a million - Mom

Prologue

Hello, my name is Nikki. I have had a passion for Yorkies my whole life. I started breeding them in the early 2000's. I have continued to learn and grow over the years as a breeder, and I believe there is always more to learn. My dogs are not "working dogs," they are a part of my family, fed high quality diets, and loved beyond words. Over the years of raising Yorkies, I did a lot of research in addition to lots of experience and hands on learning. I have mentored countless breeders. I run several groups on Facebook as well as maintaining a list of Reputable Breeders by State. Many come to me for advice and wisdom, which I love to share and help others succeed. I put my whole heart and soul into my babies and my work as a breeder and enjoy helping others do the same. My dogs are never crated, and they ARE our family, and are treated as such. Many say Yorkies are not a breed to own when you have kids. I say the exact opposite; however, don't confuse that with carelessness. It can be an amazing experience to raise them together and help them understand one another. It does require proper discipline and boundaries. These are not dogs (I don't believe any are, but especially the Yorkie) that can handle kids jumping at them, pulling their hair, etc.)

Table of Contents

History

Where did the Yorkshire Terrier come from?

Contrary to popular belief, the Yorkshire Terrier was actually first born in Scotland in the mid 1800's. Many believe they came from England, which is partially true as the breed was considered to be perfected there and it is how they got their name (eventually, after a name change). Yorkies made their first appearance in Yorkshire, England in 1861, right around the time the American Civil War began. This is where the breed was considered to be "perfected." At the time, they were known as the "Broken Haired Scotch Terrier." They were later referred to as the Toy Terrier. The Yorkie finally was given the official name as the Yorkshire Terrier in 1874.

Photo: Ginger of Crystal Divine Yorkies

They were originally bred for the purpose of hunting rats, mice, and other rodents and pests. They were also used for hunting and chasing animals such as foxes by burrowing underground. The Yorkie was very skilled at hunting down animals that lived in dens and burrows hidden on the forest floor. Hunters would carry the Yorkie in their pockets as they headed out to hunt for these animals.The burrowing type of animals can become very aggressive to defend themselves and especially their young. The Yorkshire Terrier became well known for their bravery and courage to go do such things without hesitation.

Photo: Wednesday produced by Crystal Divine Yorkies

The original Yorkies were bigger than the Yorkies we know and love today. Today, they are one of the most popular breeds of dogs as pets, and they are also one of the smallest dog breeds in the world.

They were all originally bred from Scotch Terriers (these are dogs that were from Scotland, not the breed we know and love today as the Scotch Terrier). The exact breeds that were used are not known due to the fact that these records weren't kept in these days. The name Yorkshire Terrier was given to them on account of their being improved so much in Yorkshire, England.

Health and Life Expectancy

The lifespan of a Yorkie has varied throughout the years. It can range anywhere from 13–20 years on average. Undersized Yorkies (as some refer to as Teacup, Micro, Micro Teacup, etc.) generally have a shorter life span, as they are especially prone to health problems as well as chronic diarrhea and vomiting. They are also more sensitive to anesthesia, and are very easily injured compared to a standard sized Yorkie. This is not to say that the little ones do not make great pets, but more to educate prospective owners on the proper care and

Photo: Pebbles of Crystal Divine Yorkies

ownership. They need a lot more care and attention than a standard sized Yorkie will.

Appearance

Traditional Yorkie Puppies are born with a black and tan coat and their coat can change over the years. Their hair is glossy, fine, and silky and they have a small head. Their head is more flat than round. Their ears are V-Shaped and should be erect, and set high on their head. Their tail is probably docked, in some cases they are not. In either situation, the tail should be slightly higher than their back. Looks may vary by dog, this is a basic overview of the general appearance per most show standards. For example, if you

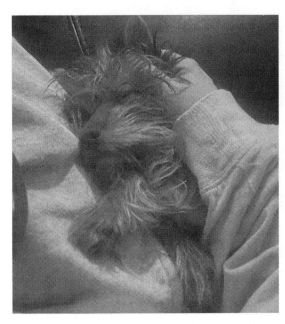

Photo: Mocha of Crystal Divine Yorkies

you have a Yorkie whose ears do not stand, this is not a deciding factor on his or her Purebred status, etc. You will read more about this a little bit later on.

Personality

Photo: Luna of Crystal Divine Yorkies

The typical Yorkie has a very lively personality; however, personality traits will differ, as they are very personable dogs. It is not uncommon to have one Yorkie who is shy and timid and another who is outgoing and wild. In general, Yorkies are very intelligent and extremely courageous dogs.

Of 132 breeds tested on average working dogs, the Yorkshire Terrier ranked 27th place for Intelligence [ref Dr. Stanley Coren, expert on Animal Intelligence].

They are quick to pick their "person," and when they do, that will forever be their "person." Even if they are rehomed, that person will always be a big piece of their heart, although they will re-adjust. They feel all emotions deeply and they love with their whole heart. They will cry when

they are sad, grieving, etc. and they always instinctively know when you need a hug. Their personality will differ (based on the dog), more than some breeds as they follow vibes of their surroundings. They are very intuitive, and most will portray a more nervous and anxious personality when their owner is not present. They rely more of the energy of their owner's presence than

Photo: Paris of Crystal Divine Yorkies

having to be physically "on their lap." They may like to be held and loved, but as long as you are present, they are happy.

They have very bold personalities and in most cases, they will be (or try to be) the "Alpha." Their instinct will always tell them to protect, and they are extremely confident, sometimes even too confident for their size. It is recommended to keep them leashed outdoors for this reason, although they are great with walking directly with their owner when directed to (until they see an animal or feel threatened).

Intelligence

Yorkies are very intelligent dogs and actually scored as

higher than average intelligence over several studies; however, they are also very selective listeners. They may not want you to know it at times, but they truly understand everything you say to them. It is good for their growth and development to communicate with them often, just as you would a human.

Some may call it silly, but you will see how fast your baby grows and develops as compared to dogs who are not talked to or dogs who are

Photo: Paris of Crystal Divine Yorkies

treated as if they do not understand. This is the same concept as reading to babies and even plants. They understand you and it keeps them learning and proves higher intelligence in their future as compared to not.

It typically takes about 15 repetitions to teach a Yorkie a command, which is quite impressive for a small breed dog. Yorkies are often taught things such as "get the paper," or to grab a specific color or name of a toy from their toy box. In my

case, I ask one of my girls to go wake up "name of child," for school, one at a time by name and she does this with

Photo: Paris of Crystal Divine Yorkies

kisses, on command and by name (Francine - pictured on Prologue page). My boy smiles on command, and uses this against me if he gets into something (Gizmo - pictured "smiling," on the cover), he will look at me and smile, so it is hard to be upset with him. Yorkies know their family members and most objects by name. They pick up very easily on titles, but selective hearing will prove how fast they will learn "dinner," or "treat," as compared to "bed," or "bath," or especially "vet."

Human Food Do's and Dont's

There are some human foods that are good and healthy

Photo: Gizmo of Crystal Divine Yorkies

snacks for your little one, and some that are no good. Certain human foods can even be fatal when consumed by a dog, such as an onion, chocolate, or grapes. I will include some examples but as always, do not experiment with other foods and your pet. Always talk with your vet before introducing any new foods. I will not be held liable if you did so against my advice.

Here are a **few** examples:

There are so many, I could go on for days. Please be mindful that new research happens all of the time. I do not in any way guarantee these and a **good rule of thumb for literally EVERYTHING you feed your dog is to ask your vet and research.** I say both because it is best to be sure. Remember when researching, **your research is only as good as the source it came from.**

Photo: Bailey of Crystal
Divine Yorkies

Yes
-Carrots
-Cucumbers
-celery
-green beans
-peas
-asparagus
-peanuts
-bread (in moderation)
-coconut or coconut water
-cashews (in moderation)
-cheese (small to moderate quantities)
-cooked pasta (in moderation)
-cooked zucchini or squash
-corn
-boiled potatoes or sweet potatoes with skin removed
-unseasoned chicken, turkey, or beef (cooked NO BONES!!!)
-apples

-bananas

-blueberries

-canteloupe

-eggs (cooked)

-green beans

-honey

-kiwi

-fish (cooked, unseasoned, no bones)

-mango

-oatmeal

-peaches

-peanut butter (with real sugar)

-pears

-pumpkin

-rice

-cottage cheese

-yogurt

-broccoli

-spinach

-strawberries

-blueberries

-air popped and plain popcorn no kernels

Photo: Paris and Mocha of Crystal Divine Yorkies

Photo: Wednesday produced by Crystal Divine Yorkies

No

-Onions

-Grapes

-cinnamon

-raisins
-tomatoes (especially the plant, toxic)
-chives
-salty or sugary snacks
-limes
-grapefruit
-lemons
-almonds
-Chocolate
-anything with salt or seasoning
-avocado
-fat trimmings
-macadamia nuts
-xylitol sugar substitute (candy, peanut butter, etc.)
-potato skins
-yeast, raw dough, moldy food
-garlic (used to be an old wives tail to kill fleas; however, this was later proven to be more harmful than good as it is part of the onion family)
-mushrooms
-gum
-caffeine

Photo: Pebbles of Crystal Divine Yorkies

Photo: Mocha of Crystal Divine Yorkies

-grapefruit
-citrus rinds
-fruit pits (apricot, peach, plum, cherry, nectarine, etc.)
-popcorn kernels
-rhubarb

Photo: Josie produced by Crystal Divine Yorkies

I have heard mixed answers from reputable sources on ham and pork. That being said, I say best to be safe than sorry and do not feed any type of pork. I have heard it is extremely hard to digest and not safe for dogs and I have recently read [AKC] that is is good and digestible, after many years of being told by different professionals that it is not. Could be a result of new research; however, I will not take the chance with my babies.

Please be sure that whatever decisions you are making are educated when it comes to feeding your Yorkie any type of human food. Remember they have very sensitive digestive systems and any and all new foods should be cleared with your vet.

Just because they can have things does not mean large amounts of any human food are okay, but an occasional treat sometimes is good. Some choose to make their foods, there are whole books on the proper nutrition for those who may be interested in learning.

Plants and Pets

Photo: Josie produced by Crystal Divine Yorkies

Plants are a staple in most American homes, both indoor and outdoor. That is why it is so important to understand that some are extremely poisonous, and can even be fatal, to pets. For example, a tomato plant can be fatal to pets. This does not only apply to fruit and vegetable plants, but often houseplants can do more harm than good and cause a very expensive trip to an emergency vet. Next time you want to buy that pretty house plant or even send a beautiful arrangement to a pet owner friend, it would be wise to research. I recommend researching each plant individually whether through a plant app, professional, or reputable source....

Photo: Bam produced by Crystal
Divine Yorkies

and always remember, **your research is only as good as the
source it came from.**

Color and Genetics

It is rumored that colored Yorkies are a result of mutt and/
or inbreeding, and it is also believed that they can "only
come in black and tan." There is NO record of any Yorkie,
EVER, being bred to a White, Chocolate, or Parti Colored
dog to create these colors, nor do any of these breeds

appear in the historical DNA of a Parti or Colorful Yorkie. DNA results from companies can throw many owners off; however, the Breed analysis result is for entertainment purposes only. DNA can not accurately predict a breed, and the best reference is your pedigree. You can refer to the fine print in any of the testing services for the terms and conditions.

Photo: Diamond, produced by Crystal Divine Yorkies

Photo: Reese of Crystal Divine Yorkies

Actually, proven through Science and Genetics, colorful Yorkies are a result of genes and how these unique colors have been hidden in the Yorkie breed for years before they were ever discovered, similar to the findings of Mr. and Mrs. Biewer, which is how Biewer a La Pom Pon was recognized in the first place with the first Parti Colored Yorkie.

Photo: Bailey of Crystal Divine Yorkies

This was a case where 2 purebred Yorkies had a puppy born white with black and brown markings, later called the Biewer a la Pom Pon. Today, in America, we refer to this more often as a Parti Yorkie, while some European lines are still called a Biewer Terrier for short. In the breeding and farming days, records were not kept on breeding stock as they are today so we may never know how far back each color actually does go, we only know what has been recorded.

Why does this not happen more often?

Because....genetics!

Genetics work in a funny way and can take many years to even remotely understand. In order to produce a Yorkie of Color, the same rare Recessive Gene for that particular

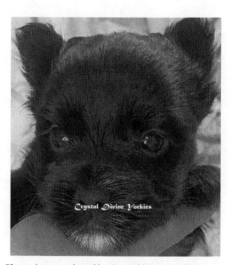

Photo: Izzy, produced by Crystal Divine Yorkies

color must be carried by both parents (this is an example that is true in SOME cases - not all genes are Recessive - not all genes require two copies). Before the genes were known, studied, or understood, it was not as easy to purposefully create these colors; thus, why they came by accident and were later confirmed through Science. As every human has a unique DNA makeup, as does a Yorkshire Terrier. For example, if

you have female Black and Tan Yorkie, who carries the recessive gene for a Chocolate Yorkie in her DNA and you breed her to a Male Black and Tan Yorkie who carries the Parti gene in his DNA, you will have a litter of Traditional Yorkie Puppies. If you breed her to a Male KB Midnight Black Yorkie (a dominant gene and also because he IS A KB Midnight Black), you will then have KB Midnight Black Yorkies;

Photo: Kash, produced by Crystal Divine Yorkies

however, for her to have Chocolate or Parti colored puppies , she and the Sire MUST both carry the Chocolate and/or Parti Recessive Gene. Through research, quality breeders, and genetic color research, many beautiful colors have been recognized. Because of the genetics and genes, these are very rare, Exotic Yorkies. The color production based on genetic profiles are a very skilled practice in which few have mastered; thus, why the cost of these breeds are so high and in demand.

With all this being said, this does not mean there could not be breeders out there who are mixing in other breeds to get certain colors in their program. It is also good to remember that your Pedigree is only as good as

Photo: Ava, produced and still owned by Crystal Divine Yorkies

the breeder it came from. Unfortunately, unethical breeders are out there, from back yard breeders to mixing breeds, falsifying paperwork, etc. Always research the breeder you plan to purchase from before buying. Ask for a buyer reference or two. Most are happy to share.

This is a very basic description of Yorkie Genetics. I go much more into detail in the Breeder's Edition version of this book. In the Breeder's Edition, I go through start to finish running a successful program, neonatal care, liver water, weaning diarrhea and osmolality, birthing, weekly puppy care, some genetic definitions, info on each Locus and how they work genetically, blue born, greying gene, Cleft Palete, and much more.

Fun Facts

* The Yorkshire Terrier does not have fur. They have hair, with a texture very similar to humans.
* One Yorkie was a War Hero. Read about Smoky and his story with his owner in World War II. It truly is an amazing story
* Of 132 breeds tested on average working dogs, the Yorkshire Terrier ranked 27th place [ref. Dr. Stanley Coren, expert on Animal Intelligence].
* Yorkies were originally bred to hunt mice and rats
* The Yorkie was first named The Broken Haired Scottish Terrier, and was renamed a decade later to Yorkshire

Photo: Athena, produced by Crystal Divine Yorkies

because although the first one was actually born in Scotland, they were actually perfected in England

- The first ever Therapy Dog was a Yorkie, this was the same dog as the War Hero, Smoky
- They were actually born in Scotland. In the mid 1800's, the Weavers brought them to England where the breed was perfected. They began appearing in shows in 1861.
- Yorkies change markings and/or colors throughout their lives
- When Yorkies were first bred, they were not as small as they are today
- A Yorkshire Terrier lived in the White House. President Richard Nixon kept one as a pet, named Pasha
- The smallest dog in recorded history was a Yorkshire Terrier. Sylvia was 2.5 inches tall, 3.5 inches long, and weighed only 4 ounces

Photo: Vivie, produced by Crystal Divine Yorkies

- They are fearless and do not run from animals bigger than them
- Yorkies are the smallest of the Terrier group
- Yorkies are the 6th most popular dog in the United States [ref American Kennel Club]
- The Yorkshire Terrier breed standard began with Huddersfield Ben, a famous Yorkie and stud owned by

Photo: Freya, produced by Crystal Divine Yorkies

Marry Ann Foster. He is still often referred to as the father of the breed to this day

* Yorkies are prone to a large number of genetic defects. When shopping for a Yorkie, it is important to be sure the breeder uses appropriate testing.

* There are actual "Yorkshire Terrier Gatherings," in New York City
* They were introduced to North America in 1872
* When properly groomed and left uncut, the Yorkie coat can grow up to 2 feet long
* They have longer life expectancies than most other breeds. The oldest Yorkshire Terrier's name was Jack. He lived to be 26 years old

- In 1984, 2 purebred Yorkshire Terriers created an accidental white Yorkie with brown and black markings. The owners were Mr. and Mrs. Biewer. The "breed," was named Biewer (pronounced like Beaver) a la Pom Pon, later referred to as the Parti Yorkie in America. The Biewer is now recognized as its own breed through the American Kennel Club in 2014, although technically it is still a purebred Yorkshire Terrier.
- A Yorkie's Tongue is actually longer than his (or her) mouth. That is why some wonder why they are always sticking them out or showing them, or even curling them at times.

Photo: Brooklyn, produced by Crystal Divine Yorkies

Yorkie Care

When your puppy comes home from his or her breeder to your loving home, he or she will be at least 8 weeks old (in most cases. Any younger than this is unethical and illegal

in most States. With their small size, a breeder may even decide to keep a puppy a little bit longer, depending on a number of things such as how he or she is eating on his or her own, his or her weight, proper socialization and life skills, etc.

While some buyers may be disappointed when these decisions are made, it is the ultimate best interest of your

Photo: Bailey of Crystal Divine Yorkies

new puppy. Although the puppy has been determined by the breeder to be ready to go home, it is still very important to remember they are still very new to the world. You will be responsible for teaching them important life skills. They will very often look to you when they are unsure of how to behave or react to a certain situation.

Food

Yorkie puppies require a well balanced diet, as this is the foundation for good health. It is **STRONGLY recommended to stick to the recommendation made by your breeder**, assuming you've chosen a good reputable breeder to work with...unless otherwise medically necessary to switch according to your Veterinarian. Some breeders even require this in order to keep the Health Guarantee in good standing. If you do decide it is absolutely necessary to make a change in the diet, you do not want to do so at such a young age, and when you do, a proper Transition

Photo: Luna of Crystal Divine Yorkies

will be required. This is because Yorkies have a very sensitive digestive system, and a fast changeover can cause upset stomach, diarrhea, nausea, and many other issues.

If you need to transition, it is recommended to mix the two foods and over the course of 3 to 4 weeks. Start with 90% what the Yorkie is used to and 10% what you are switching to and slowly increase the amount of new food to the mix each day.

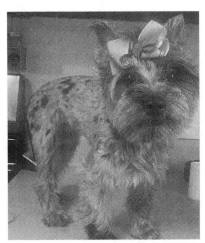

Photo: Luna of Crystal Divine Yorkies

Free Feeding - the method of having food out and readily accessibly by your pet at all times throughout the day, providing them the opportunity to eat whenever they are hungry.

Yorkie puppies should be free fed up until at least the age of 3 months old. They are known to be grazers and not great eaters when expected to eat a meal at a time. Although your Breeder probably recommended no more than 1/4 cup 3 times per day, this is also accurate, and it is to avoid things such as puppy bloat that could happen if you are not mindful. Free feed, but only if you don't have an "over eater." While it may sound confusing, the simple answer is...Free feed, but no more than the average amount advised by your breeder or vet. This helps to prevent the puppy from going too long without sustenance which can cause a dangerous drop in blood sugar levels, which can cause hypoglycemia. At the same time, if your puppy seems to be overeating, reach out to your breeder or vet for further feeding advice.

You may need to remind a young puppy where his/her food and water dishes are for the first few weeks and always make sure he/she is drinking a good amount of water.

When your puppy is about 3-4 months old, you may want to start giving him scheduled meals 3 times per day.

Photo: Freya produced by Crystal Divine Yorkies

Although free feeding is preferred, if that seems to work for your Yorkie, that would be the time to make that decision. If you do decide not to free feed, please remember that a Yorkie puppy will not eat very much and it really is best to spread the food out from morning til evening. You can also give some small snacks, but it is recommended to reserve these as rewards for housebreaking since they will mean more if the puppy is hungry for it. Also be sure not to over-reward with treats. As far as treats, I strongly recommend the mini treats such as Cesars. When deciding on bones, the most important thing to be sure of is **NO RAWHIDE**. This is not easy to digest and could cause a number of health problems, and could even lead to surgical intervention, or even death. In my program, I feed and require my buyers to feed Health Extension Little bites, unless

otherwise recommended by a Vet. The QR Code on this page will take you directly to my recommendation as well as save you 10% when ordering.

Photo: Wednesday produced by Crystal Divine Yorkies

Socialization

The 2-4 month old timeframe is a very important time for socialization. Your pup will look to you to show them the ways of life, how to react to things and what types of behaviors are or are not expected. Your puppy should continue to be socialized, as they were started with their breeder. Please see the Socialization checklist for more advice on this. It is available in your Resources at the end of this book.

Photo:, Pebbles of Crystal Divine Yorkies

A Yorkie puppy should be exposed to normal household noises; however a very noisy or overstimulating home is not best for your puppy until they are more accustomed to their surroundings. Allow your pup to slowly become used to their environment while maintaining proper socialization. You'll thank me later :).

VERY IMPORTANT: DO NOT BRING YOUR YORKIE PUPPY OUTSIDE AT ALL until all puppy shots are given. This includes public places where there are any dogs or even where any dogs may have been. Yes, even use caution in the Vet waiting area. Although most are clean and well kept, puppies are very sensitive and are more at risk than the average dog. When you take your puppy

outside too soon, there is a high risk of contracting things like Parvovirus, which can be fatal, and there are windows of vulnerability in which the antibodies passed down from the dam are weak but the full protection from the inoculations are not at full strength. You will read more about puppy immunity and how it fades when weaning a little bit

Photo: Bandit produced by Crystal Divine Yorkies

later on (in the Breeder's Edition). This is a result of weening from mom's milk to puppy food. Puppy food does not provide the same immunities that are provided by mom early on.

Just like caring for a baby, spending time and holding your puppy is very important. At times, they would rather run around and simply be a puppy, but you will catch moments when he or she wants to be held. These moments will increase with age and maturity, or sometimes even vary by personality. This is very important for bonding, trust, and development. If you are having trouble, try again in small bits.

I talk more about puppy socialization for Breeders in the Breeder's Edition of this book.

Touch the entire body to help a pup become accustomed to what will soon be a full grooming and brushing, which he or she should have had an introduction to with the breeder. Touch the mouth and teeth to prepare him or her dental cleanings with a canine toothbrush sized for toy breeds and a quality toothpaste. There is more info on this on the

Photo:, Bruno produced by Crystal Divine Yorkies Socialization guide as well.

Sleep

Young Yorkie puppies sleep a lot. A Yorkshire Terrier puppy will sleep about 15 hours per day on average and can even sleep as much as 18. Make sure he or she has a nice comfortable place to sleep. When investing in a bed, be careful to stay away from the little inexpensive ones. Yorkies are known to chew them apart and take the stuffing out.

They will sleep as you hold them, and take many cat naps throughout the day. They are even considered to seep a lot as they age into thriving adults. Many of us are not able to count the number of times we "could not move," because our Yorkie was just so comfortably sleeping on us.

Medical

When you buy from a reputable breeder, your puppy has most likely had the vaccinations required for his or her age. Unfortunately, that is not always the case. This is one of many reasons to only buy from a reputable breeder and stay far away from places like big name pet stores, puppy mills, and back yard breeders.

If you got a free or "cheaper," puppy from the internet, puppy mill, the average "cheaper puppy," or from a bug name pet shop (not recommend, as most of those puppies come from Puppy Mills, and some remain to be treated as such) it is best to assume that no shots

Photo:, Aladdin produced by Crystal Divine Yorkies

have been given and start at the very beginning, unless you have been given proper documentation.

What about rescues? Although most do vaccinate, it is best to be sure. Never assume that any dog is up-to-date without proof on paper, even from a reputable breeder.

It's very important that your puppy gets all of the age appropriate shots and deworming treatments in order to protect him or her from possible parasites and/or fatal diseases. He or she will not be ready to take walks in the park or to be brought to any area (stores, outside, etc) that other dogs may have been until all puppy shots have been

Photo:, Chance produced by Crystal Divine Yorkies

given, which will be at least 16 weeks of age AND a clearance from your vet.

When your puppy comes home, even from a reputable breeder, he or she will need a "new puppy," vet appointment. The sooner the better, as the change can cause stress from moving which can cause coccidia, ear infections, etc. - even after being properly cared for and well loved and spoiled during their time with their breeder. These can be caused simply from the stress of being separated from mom and moving homes.

Photo:,Mocha of Crystal Divine Yorkies

I talk more about Medical care, especially Neonatal Medical Care - in the Breeder's Edition of this book.

The vet can do an exam and check for any potential problems. If purchasing from a reputable breeder, you will usually be asked to bring your new Yorkie puppy to the vet within a certain amount of time (usually within the first week, and advised that the sooner the better) to confirm that the pup is healthy and doing well even after their transition to their new home. This is normally a requirement of your agreement to the health guarantee in the contract.

Grooming

Yorkies are very high maintenance dogs. They require daily brushing and lots of grooming. This will include bath time (which can begin by the time your new puppy comes home, as instructed by your breeder) , brushing, ear care, nail care, paw trimming, coat trimmings and more. It is also suggested to use grooming time to check for any early signs of health issues. If using a professional groomer, it is highly recommended to look for a groomer that is not just experienced in "grooming dogs," but you want one very educated and experienced in Yorkie grooming. This is important because Yorkies don't have "fur," like most dogs do. They have "hair." There is a big difference in how it should be cut and maintained. Your best bet is always to find a Yorkie specific groomer who is well experienced in the breed and its grooming needs.

Photo:,Ivy produced by Crystal Divine Yorkies

Having a rotation system helps with grooming time and helps keep things interesting for your puppy, rather than forming a love hate relationship every time they see the brush. For example, brush every day but maybe do paws one day, face another day, ears another day, etc. until your puppy is more used to the process. Teach him or her to enjoy it. Be sure to brush your Yorkie every day. Follow your Vet's recommendations for dental care, etc. and whether you use a groomer or do a full groom yourself, you should groom every 3-4 weeks.

This applies to the average adult Yorkie, and could always be more or less. Puppies require a weekly grooming on average. I talk a lot about the grooming process in young puppies, and the weekly appropriate routines in the Breeder's Edition of this book. I also talk about Ears and different methods to helping them look great!

Photo:,puppies produced by Crystal Divine Yorkies

They will need their eyes wiped every morning with a lukewarm clean wet rag. This helps clean up the "sleep," from the night. Some Yorkies get messy eyes more than others and need cleaned up more often. If you're noticing it is too often, it could very well be the food or water your dog or puppy is drinking. Try switching to distilled water. If this does not help after a couple weeks, talk with your vet and your breeder to discuss possible diet changes. More than likely, it is a slight allergy to the main protein source in the food, but could be a number of other things as well, usually sourced from an allergy - even a slight allergy in which this is the only symptom.

Toys

Yorkie puppies will need both play toys and chew toys to help with teething. Talk to your vet about which chew and teething toys are recommended. Personally, I love Unstuffed Animals for my program and so do my dogs. Yorkies have a tendency to tear the stuffing out of stuffed toys and leave it all over the house; not to mention the

Photo:,Koda produced by Crystal Divine Yorkies

choking hazard of the contents.

Puzzles are great entertainment, as well as Interactive bones and toys. My dogs have a "hide the squirrel tree," and a "hide the treat snail puzzle," that seem to be popular choices around here. The unstuffed toys seem to be the favorite, they actually each have their "baby," - the toy they will not share. Providing an adequate amount of appropriate chew toys also helps to slow down the household item chewing while they are

Photo:,Ava produced by and owned by Crystal Divine Yorkies

still learning.

A lot of chewing is due to teething. As far as teething, please know that Ice cubes are not good for Yorkies and have even lead to hospitalization.

While toys are great and our dogs love them, they can also fill with dirt and germs very fast. Make sure to wash dog toys regularly. I have a system where I keep a bin of toys out at a time and wash and rotate at least once a week, unless needed more often. Remember, these go inside their mouthes. It is very important to keep them clean as it is a great passageway for unwanted germs.

A Safe and Happy Home

Puppy-proofing your home is very important, just like baby proofing for a human. Plug outlet covers, no small objects laying around, secure wires and plugs, and checking for health and safety hazards will become your daily routine. Little Yorkies are big explorers, especially and even more so when they are teething! They are very curious, remember they were bred for hunting and ratting, they are meant to be explorers. Be sure to avoid cords, plugs, wires, —-or literally ANYTHING they can fit in their mouth that is not meant for them, on the floor or any place that can be reached. These can usually be tied up and hidden behind

appliances or even taped down in situations when it is

unavoidable to have them out. Keep low plug outlets covered with protectors. No small objects on the floor should be an enforced rule. Choking is a great hazard and is very real. It is very avoidable and if let go, can even lead to death. While the list can go on all day, it is also very important to mention to **beware of toxic substances**. The most commonly found items right at the level at which a young pup can reach are soap, cleaning supplies, alcoholic beverages, cigarettes (nicotine poisoning is fatal), etc. Chocolate is also a big hazard that can be fatal (as can onions and a number of other things you will see on your no-no list later on in Human food Do's and Dont's).

Remember when I said that preparing for a Yorkie Puppy is very similar to child-proofing your home or office for a baby? It might be harder...they can get under furniture and in and out of places we can not. Regularly check for

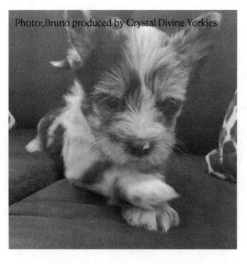
Photo: Bruno produced by Crystal Divine Yorkies

anything that could be put in their mouth. **A general rule of thumb is that is they can fit it in their mouth, they will...and if you think they can't, they will probably prove you wrong.** Watch for items such as: keys, dentures, glasses, remotes, shoes and laces, bills and coins, hair accessories, etc.

It is important to note that very small dog breeds such as the Yorkie can be easily injured when jumping off of furniture. When they come home at 8 weeks old, their bones in their knees are not even fused all the way together yet, which will change in time as they grow. It is HIGHLY suggested to have dog steps or ramps from your bed, couch, or other furniture - to the floor if your little one has a habit of jumping up and then down. If not, you will want to be sure to train your puppy to not jump or climb onto objects that leaping down from may be harmful to the knees and/or hips.

While you may read and understand everything written in this book, you can not assume that others around you share that same knowledge or heard that same advice.

Photo:, Dash produced by Crystal Divine Yorkies

Crystal Divine Yorkies

Have a family meeting so that everyone in the home understands the importance of always being aware of what is going on. Have a safety plan. Educate your family as it is important everyone understands the breed well, especially when it comes to watching out for them. They are too brave and careless to pay much attention to where your feet will go next when they are running around. It is surprising how many little dogs are injured (usually severely) when an owner accidental steps or trips over them. Trauma, including being dropped or stepped on, is one of the leading causes of death for puppies of any breed, so imagine the severity when it is just a little Yorkie.

Exercise

Yorkies are very energetic dogs and need a place or a plan

Photo:, Chloe produced by Crystal Divine Yorkies

to release their energy. Failure to do so can lead to a number of behavioral problems, all of which that are avoidable with appropriate with proper exercise.

There is a fine line between providing enough activity for good health and overworking your Yorkie, which can also lead to health issues and possible problems with growth plate development. Talk to your vet about what is or is not a good exercise plan for your dog. This is not to say do not let the dog run around with the "puppy zoomies," because you are afraid of over exercise.

All puppies need exercise on a regular basis. It is a way for them to release their energy. A good example is about a 15-20 minute walk twice a day in addition to the "zoomies" they get around the house. Fenced in yards with room to

Photo:, Ava, produced by and owned by Crystal Divine Yorkies

run are great - but **do not ever leave a Yorkie outside unattended.** There are many predators such as hawks, owls, foxes, coyotes, etc. that are known to come by and take Yorkies and leave. It happens so fast but if you are outside with them, they are less likely to try, and/or you will see them coming in time to act or pick up your baby.

Remember that getting out of the house to go for a walk is not the same type of exercise as zooming around the house. It is necessary for a puppy (of appropriate age to be outside) to get fresh air as well as the opportunity to see new things and become accustomed to sidewalks, other people, and other dogs (as long as they are old enough, in good health, and medically fit to do so). Taking the time and patience it takes to teach your puppy to walk on leash will go a long way in establishing yourself as leader, which helps a Yorkie mature into a well-behaved dog. Remember, they DO understand you; however, they are very selective

listeners and may need lots of positive reinforcement, especially in early training.

Photo:, Bailey of Crystal Divine Yorkies

Shaking

Yorkies, among many other small breeds, are known to shake at times. It was once believed to always be a result of Hypoglycemia; however, it could be a number of things. It is important to know and understand what you are looking for when trying to figure out why he or she is shaking.

Photo:, Jasper, produced by Crystal Divine Yorkies

Some refer to this as trembling or shivering. It could last for a few seconds or could even last longer, until someone makes some sort of change that calms the shaking down.

Some Yorkies have been known shake for seemingly no reason. While this can be the case, it is never safe to just assume that it is the case...it is always best to be sure first. Most importantly, **keep your vet informed**. Sometimes Yorkies will begin to shake for a number of different reasons. Some of the common reasons your Yorkie may shake are very easily fixed at home:

Body Temperature

Yorkie temperatures run higher than that of a Human. To us, they may seem fine - but to them, they could be freezing cold. Keep a thermometer nearby in your medical kits to get an accurate reading on this if needed. This is especially common in Yorkies. A lot of dog breeds have double coats which work together to provide insulation and help regulate body temperature. Many other dog

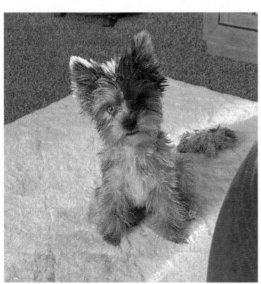

Photo:, Freya, produced by Crystal Divine Yorkies

breeds also have fur (double composition). The Yorkie has a single coat, and rather than fur - the Yorkie has hair (single composition). This means that Yorkies are not as protected so it is important to be careful during chilly weather, cold rain, or even a chilly room in the house. Don't spend too much time outdoors in the winter, especially if you live where it gets particularly cold or snowy.

Remember that a Yorkie will feel the cold much more than dog breeds with a double coat or even breeds with a single coat of fur, as it is twice as thick as hair, making the follicles much thicker than that of a Yorkie. Yorkie puppies will feel the cold a lot more than any adult will - sometimes this can get very dangerous and also why it is so important to be educated in the matter. In the Breeder's Edition of this book, you will see a guide of temperatures in which puppies need to be kept by age. This is a good reference to go by when checking temperatures of your puppy. Adult dogs temperatures range slightly higher than humans. Usually from about 100.5 to about 102.5.

Photo:, Savanah Jane, produced by Crystal Divine Yorkies

Shivering is a common reflex that can happen when a dog's body reacts to the cold. The core body temperature drops

below their normal range (normal ranges can vary by breed), which results in shivering, which is actually a reflex of the Yorkie's body - or its way or warming up. Although this may happen with any Yorkies, it is more common at a young or even a particularly old age.

Photo:, Asher, produced by Crystal Divine Yorkies

This is not to say it can't happen at any age - remember this is a very sensitive breed.

Even though you may feel warm, your Yorkie is much smaller than you and may begin shaking due to even the slightest drop in temperature. Remember, their average body temperatures are higher than ours. This is even more common when your Yorkie is wet, whether it is from the rain, bath, snow, etc. If you want to prevent shivering when your Yorkie is wet, wrap him or her in a towel and cuddle him or her until they warm up, if you have a fire place - relax by the fire (safely - obviously) with him or her for a while all cuddled up. You can let your him or her down to do the "dog shake" to remove excess water.

It is assumed by many that people dress their Yorkies and that is "not right," or "torture," or "high maintenance," or the list goes on....

 Actually, this can help a lot to keep them warm, especially on a cool or rainy day. Anything from a light t-shirt to a rain coat or a warm winter jacket would be appropriate, depending on your dog and the temperature he or she is around. This is a lot of the reason why many of our Yorkies have a regular wardrobe and have certain things they wear certain places, or even a selection of coats by weather type. My Yorkies even have Snuggies :).

Hypoglycemia

Hypoglycemia is a result of a drop in blood sugar levels. This is very common in Yorkies and small dogs and while sometimes this can be fixed easily if you are educated in the matter. In severe cases - this can be fatal... especially for very young puppies.

What causes this?

For young Yorkshire Terrier puppies, often it can "just happen," or it could be caused by stress (transitioning to a new home, being introduced to too many new environments, overstimulation or

Photo: Pebbles of Crystal Divine Yorkies

situations in a shorter amount of time than average) or a fast change in diet, as discussed earlier on, or even being fed a diet that is not of good quality. This is not to say in any way to say that a puppy should not be introduced to new things. As you read earlier on, **socialization is a very important part of healthy development and leads to a well behaved Yorkie**. Just remember that fine line we talked about. However, puppies can become overwhelmed and may need to slow down at times.

Hypoglycemia can also be caused by going long periods of time without food. For a Yorkie, a long time is longer than it may seem for us. This is also one of the main reasons we always recommend free feeding up to at least 3-4 months, if not much longer. Please do not be that person that essentially "starves," their Yorkie just to have the "smallest one." While a small Yorkie is cute, each of these risks are more than doubled - not to mention proper nutrition is essential to their development.

Photo: Lilly, now Brooklyn produced by Crystal Divine Yorkies

When Hypoglycemia sets in, a dog will shake or shiver, just like they would if they were too cold. Other signs of Hypoglycemia may or may not present themselves, depending on the situation and the dog or puppy in question. Additional signs to look out for, which may occur at the same time or soon after, are...

weakness, dizziness, trouble walking, etc.

If Hypoglycemia is left untreated, a dog can slip into a coma and the result could even be fatal.

Because of the risk of Hypoglycemia in small breed dogs, all owners of all toy breed dogs should have Nutrical on hand. If you do not have **Nutrical**, some acceptable

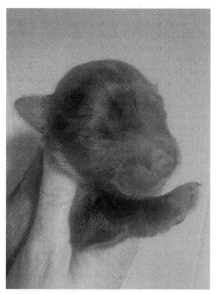

Photo:, Jasper, produced by Crystal Divine Yorkies

substitutions are Karo syrup or honey. It is best to be safe than sorry. **Keep this on hand at all times** and even a small emergency supply in the car or on you when you are out and about.

Rub a small amount directly onto the gums. This should stabilize him/her enough in order to be brought to your Vet for an exam and to check his or her sugar levels. Although you probably just solved the problem, you can not know for sure without proper blood work and vet exam so you always want to clear up the situation with a professional as well as the proper blood work to confirm the sugar was or wasn't the reason for shaking.

Fear

Fear comes in all forms. Some even call them the "Rescue shakes," or I like to refer to them as the "Ginger shakes," inspired by my sweet girl, "Ginger Snap (pictured on this

Photo:, Ginger of Crystal Divine Yorkies

page)." She does not like the vet so she would just sit there and shake. She even started doing this every car ride in fear of going to the vet. Her vet said she is just a shaky dog, despite all of her blood panels and testing which came back great. They even started to use the term "Ginger shakes." It took about a year and a half to break this habit. The lesson in this is that like humans, Yorkies each have their own personality. You must learn what your dog does not like or is afraid of, or if they simply like to shake. One Yorkie may shake when going to the vet, while another may shake when they meet someone new, while their sibling does not shake for any reason, but it is always best to never assume this is the case.

How do you stop it?

Immediately stop whatever is causing your baby to shake, even if this means inconveniencing someone else. A puppy or dog that trembles due to a situation will not simply "get over it," until they feel satisfied.

This does NOT mean that you will now avoid that

situation. It does mean that you have a new item on your to do list! Remember your socialization checklist and thew importance of it. Slow bits of introduction to the "fear," is best practice. While shaking due to fear will not physically harm a dog, it does cause stress, which can lead to a

Photo:, King Kash, produced by Crystal Divine Yorkies

number or things such as coccidia or ear infections, etc. It can even harm the puppy or dog's self-esteem and/or confidence.

Excitement

Excitement is a less common reason for the "Yorkie shakes," - but also should never be underestimated. Excitement, or overexcitement is still a less popular reason that some Yorkies shake. Sometimes, they may have so much happiness and/or so much excitement that his or whole whole body can actually begin to shake in anticipation. Some even get so excited that they start to pee - this is more common in males but it does happen with females also; hence picture of my boy Prince pictured here. He had to learn this was not an acceptable way of greeting me when I come home when he was younger. This is another perfect example of proper socialization in teaching

Photo:, Prince of Crystal Divine Yorkies

them to maintain their excitement in other ways. Although a Yorkie being excited does not sound like a very "fatal situation," it is best to rule out other reasons for the

Photo:, Chloe produced by Crystal Divine Yorkies

shaking and put them to a stop. A Yorkie could still be excited while cold, etc. It is always in the best interest of your puppy to stop the shaking and be sure there is not an ongoing problem. The shaking with excitement should lessen in time with "practice." Yorkies get excited a lot :).

On behalf of all of the fur family of Crystal Divine Yorkies, thank you for reading

Love,

Pebbles and her "siblings"

Photo:, Pebbles of Crystal Divine Yorkies

Thank You

Thank you for taking the time to read this Book. There are no words to describe my Gratitude for all of you. If you enjoyed and want to keep reading about the breed, check out the Breeder's Edition.

Resources

Some of these resources can be scanned using a Scan app and simply printed.

Vet:

_____

_____

_____

Emergency Vet:

My Facebook Groups:

Most groups have Emoji's in the name - some show and some don't at times - just check for "Nikki Lee," as the Admin as many have similar names

This list is Subject to Change - check for updated list on Crystal Divine Yorkies Facebook Page

"Yorkies of America by CDY"

"Yorkie Colors and Genetics by CDY"

"Yorkies of Pennsylvania"

"Colorful Yorkies"

"Yorkies of the South"

"Yorkies of the Sunshine State, and Surrounding"

"KB Midnight Black Yorkies"

"The Beauty of Colorful Yorkies"

"Yorkies of the Carolina's"

Yorkie Studs (and Muffins)"

"Yorkies of Georgia"

"The Yorkie Life"

"Crazy Yorkie Lovers"

"Colorful Yorkie Puppies"

"Merle Yorkies"

"Yorkie Breeding and Whelping

My New Puppy Checklist:

My Socialization Checklist:

Your puppy has had a great start on proper development and socialization. Please be sure to continue working on this with him/her as well as maintaining regular vet care to ensure the best outcome for a healthy, happy puppy. I am not by any means suggesting shooting guns or doing anything dangerous next to your puppy, especially if you are untrained; however, playing the sound on a TV can encourage proper development and socialization.

SOCIALIZATION CHECKLIST

Unfamiliar People
- [ ] wearing backpacks
- [ ] people dancing
- [ ] different etnicities
- [ ] people riding a bike
- [ ] men with beards
- [ ] men with deep voices
- [ ] wearing hats
- [ ] wearing sunglasses
- [ ] toddlers
- [ ] infants
- [ ] elderly
- [ ] children playing
- [ ] people running
- [ ] tall men
- [ ] women
- [ ] clowns
- [ ] teenagers
- [ ] walking with canes or walkers

Meeting Animals
- [ ] puppies
- [ ] male adult dogs
- [ ] female adult dogs
- [ ] kittens
- [ ] cats
- [ ] horses
- [ ] pocket pets
- [ ] different breeds
- [ ] old dogs
- [ ] farm animals
- [ ] squirells
- [ ] rabbits
- [ ] birds
- [ ] cows
- [ ] flat-faced dogs
- [ ] forest animals
- [ ] ducks
- [ ] different temperaments

Visual and Noises
- [ ] sirens
- [ ] fireworks
- [ ] car horns
- [ ] motorbikes
- [ ] thunderstorms
- [ ] wheelchairs
- [ ] cars
- [ ] door bells
- [ ] skateboards
- [ ] airplanes
- [ ] vacuum cleaner
- [ ] hair dryer
- [ ] blender
- [ ] gunshot
- [ ] alarm
- [ ] trucks
- [ ] washing machine
- [ ] crowds of people

Body Handling
- [ ] check the ears
- [ ] bending towards puppy
- [ ] opening the eyelids
- [ ] grabbing the collar
- [ ] handling and trimming toenails
- [ ] hugging your puppy
- [ ] holding him in your arms
- [ ] squeezing the feet
- [ ] grooming brush
- [ ] examine mouth
- [ ] touching tail
- [ ] touching belly
- [ ] cradling the puppy in your arms

Places
- [ ] parks
- [ ] boarding kennel
- [ ] daycare
- [ ] pet store
- [ ] veterinarian
- [ ] groomer
- [ ] lake
- [ ] forest
- [ ] shopping areas
- [ ] bridges
- [ ] night time

dog friendly:
- [ ] class locations
- [ ] events
- [ ] restaurants

Objects and Flooring
- [ ] pots and pans
- [ ] brooms
- [ ] bags blowing in the wind
- [ ] umbrellas
- [ ] sidewalk signs
- [ ] garbage cans
- [ ] escalators
- [ ] bench
- [ ] balllons
- [ ] elevators
- [ ] tile floors
- [ ] wet grass
- [ ] stairs
- [ ] wood floors
- [ ] carpet

Remember your puppy CAN NOT BE OUTSIDE until 16 weeks of age and vet says okay

New Puppy Checklist

	✓
🐾 PUPPY FOOD — Royal Canin Yorkshire Terrier Puppy Food	
🐾 FOOD & DRINK BOWLS — Provided in your puppy pack	
🐾 ~~COLLAR~~/HARNESS — Collars can cause Treacheal Coppapse. Please only use a Harness	
🐾 LEASH	
🐾 ID TAG	
🐾 CRATE — Please only use for overnight during training time to ensure safety as a puppy. Yorkies are not meant to "live" in crates.	
🐾 DOG BED	
🐾 CHEW TOYS — Unstuffed Animals are the best, one is provided in your puppy pack	
🐾 POOPER SCOOPER/ POOP BAGS	
🐾 BRUSH — Wet Brush. Provided in your puppy pack.	
🐾 GROOMING WIPES — Convenient for between baths	
🐾 DOGGY TOOTHBRUSH/TOOTHPASTE	
🐾 PUPPY SHAMPOO — Provided in your puppy pack.	
🐾 NAIL CLIPPERS	
🐾 WEE WEE PADS — Washable puppy pads from Amazon. Puppies will chew the disposable puppy pads.	
🐾 STAIN REMOVER	
🐾 TREATS — Cesars Mini's are great. You will need Treats AND chew bones (NO RAWHIDE!). Some are provided in your puppy pack	

List of reputable Breeders by State:

The live list or reputable breeders by State has grown and is updated so often that it would be unfair to print its current copy as of this date. This is an ever-changing and growing list. The most recent and up to date list will always be posted in "Yorkies of America by CDY," Facebook group on the main page. If for any reason the group disappears, look for updates on "Crystal Divine Yorkies," Facebook page or send me an email: crystaldivineyorkies@icloud.com

References

1. Karlsson EK, Baranowska I, Wade CM, Salmon Hillbertz NH, Zody MC, Anderson N, Biagi TM, Patterson N, Pielberg GR, Kulbokas EJ 3rd, Comstock KE, Keller ET, Mesirov JP, von Euler H, Kampe O, Hedhammar A, Lander ES, Andersson G, Andersson L, Londblad-Toh K. Efficient mapping of mendelian traits in dogs through genome-wide association. Nat Genet. 2007 Nov; 39(11):1321-8. [PubMed: 17906626]

2. Dreger DL, Parker HG, Ostrander EA, Schmutz SM. Identification of a mutation that is associated with the saddle tan and black-and-tan phenotypes in Basset Hounds and Pembroke Welsh Corgis. J Hered. 2013 May-Jun; 104(3):399-406. [PubMed: 23519866]

3. Kerns JA, Newton J, Berryere TG, Rubin EM, Cheng JF, Schmutz SM, Barsh GS. Characterization of the dog Agouti gene and a nonagouti mutation in German Shepherd Dogs. Mamm Genome. 2004 Oct; 15(10):798-808. [PubMed: 15520882]

4. Clark LA, Wahl JM, Rees CA, Murphy KE. Retrotransposon insertion in SILV is responsible for merle patterning of the domestic dog. Proc Natl Acad Sci USA. 2006 Jan 31; 103(5):1376-81. [PubMed: 16407134]

5. Kaelin CB, Barsh GS. Genetics of pigmentation in dogs and cats. Annu. Rev. Anim. Biosci. 1:16.1-16.32 (2013).

6. Everts RE, Rothuizen J, van Oost BA. Identification of a premature stop codon in the melanocyte-stimulating hormone receptor gene (MC1R) in Labrador and Golden retrievers with yellow coat color. Animal Genetics. 2000 Jun; 31(3):194-99. [PubMed: 10895310]

7. Candille SI, Kaelin CB, Cattanach BM, Yu B, Thompson DA, Nix MA, Kerns JA, Schmutz SM, Millhauser GL, Barsh GS. A β-defensin mutation causes black coat color in domestic dogs. Science. 2007 Nov 30; 318(5855):1418-23. [PubMed: 17947548]

8. Royal Canin University. Royal Canin. 2022. [https://my.royalcanin.com].

9. American Kennel Club. The American Kennel Club, Inc. 2022. [https://www.akc.org/dog-breeds/yorkshire-terrier/].

10. Dr. Stanley Coren. Stanley Coren. 2009. [https://www.stanleycoren.com].

11. CDC. Center For Disease Control and Prevention. Storage and Handling. U.S. Department of Health & Human Services. [https://www.cdc.gov/vaccines/hcp/admin/storage/toolkit/index.html]

2. National Cancer Institute. U.S. Department of Health and Human Services. National Cancer Institute. [https://www.cancer.gov/genetics-dictionary-def]

Copyright

The most heartfelt THANK YOU!!! to all of you for reading, supporting, and for loving the Yorkie breed as we do. There are no words for my Gratitude for all who took the time to read. I hope you found all you were looking for and more, while this info may seem very basic to some. While I am sure there is a thing or two I could have elaborated more on, as I said - I could go on for days and days. I may consider another book in the future :)

-Nikki Lee

Crystal Divine Yorkies

www.CrystalDivineYorkies.com

Facebook Groups:

Most groups have Emoji's in the name - some show and some don't at times - just check for "Nikki Lee," as the Admin as many have similar names

This list is Subject to Change - check for updated list on Crystal Divine Yorkies Facebook Page

"Yorkies of America by CDY"

"Yorkie Colors and Genetics by CDY"

"Yorkies of Pennsylvania"

"Colorful Yorkies"

"Yorkies of the South"

"Yorkies of the Sunshine State, and Surrounding"

"KB Midnight Black Yorkies"

"The Beauty of Colorful Yorkies"

"Yorkies of the Carolina's"

Yorkie Studs (and Muffins)"

"Yorkies of Georgia"

"The Yorkie Life"

"Crazy Yorkie Lovers"

"Colorful Yorkie Puppies"

"Merle Yorkies"

"Yorkie Breeding and Whelping"

About the Author

Hello, my name is Nikki. I have had a passion for Yorkies my whole life. I started breeding them in the early 2000's. I have continued to learn and grow over the years as a breeder, and I believe there is always more to learn. My dogs are not "working dogs," they are a part of my family, fed high quality diets, and loved beyond words. Over the years of raising Yorkies, I did a lot of research on different color variations and have mentored countless breeders. I run several groups on Facebook as well as maintaining a list of Reputable Breeders by State. Many come to me for advice and wisdom, which I love to share and help others succeed. I put my whole heart and soul into my babies and my work as a breeder and enjoy helping others do the same. My dogs are never crated, and they ARE our family, and are treated as such. Many say Yorkies are not a breed to own when you have kids. I say the exact opposite; however, don't confuse that with carelessness. It can be an amazing experience to raise them together and help them understand one another. It does require proper discipline and boundaries. These are not dogs (I don't believe any are, but especially the Yorkie) that can handle kids jumping at them, pulling their hair, etc.)

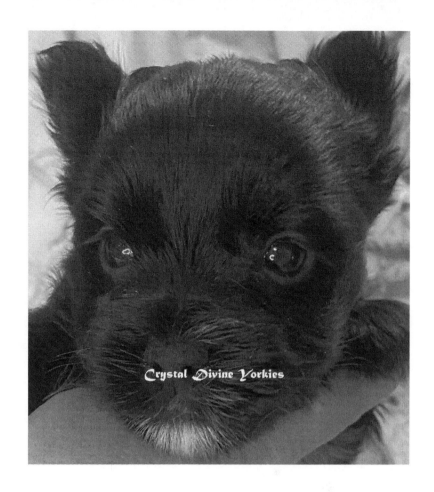

Made in the USA
Columbia, SC
13 August 2024

39990828R00045